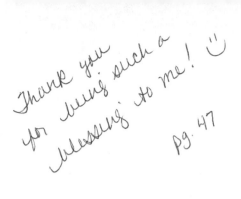

Thank you
for being such a
blessing to me! :)

pg. 47

To:

Kathy

From:

♡ Jill

Date:

12/03

Daniel 12:3

FAMILY
CHRISTIAN
PRESS

Promises, Praises & Prayers

for a

friend

Promises, Praises & Prayers

for a

friend

FAMILY
CHRISTIAN
PRESS

ISBN 1404184287

*The quoted ideas expressed in this book (but not scripture verses) are not, in
all cases, exact quotations, as some have been edited for clarity and brevity.
In all cases, the author has attempted to maintain the speaker's original
intent. In some cases, quoted material for this book was obtained from
secondary sources, primarily print media. While every effort was made to
ensure the accuracy of these sources, the accuracy cannot be guaranteed. For
additions, deletions, corrections or clarifications in future editions of this
text, please write FAMILY CHRISTIAN PRESS.*

Certain elements of this text, including quotations, stories, and selected
groupings of Bible verses, have appeared, in part or in whole, in
publications previously written by Criswell Freeman, Psy. D., these
excerpts are used with permission.

All scripture quotations, unless otherwise indicated, are taken from the HOLY BIBLE,
NEW INTERNATIONAL VERSION ©. NIV ©. Copyright © 1973, 1978, 1984, by
International Bible Society. Used by permission of Zondervan Publishing House. All
rights reserved.

Scripture taken from *THE MESSAGE.* Copyright © 1993, 1994, 1995, 1996. Used by
permission of NavPress Publishing Group.

Scripture taken from the NEW AMERICAN STANDARD BIBLE®, Copyright ©
1960, 1962, 1963, 1968, 1971, 1972, 1973, 1975, 1977, 1995 by The Lockman Foundation. Used by permission.

Scripture quotations marked (RSV) are taken from The Holy Bible, Revised Standard
Version, Copyright © 1946 Division of Christian Education of the National Council
of the Churches of Christ in the United States of America. Used by permission.

Scripture quotations marked (NKJV) are taken from The Holy Bible, New King
James Version, Copyright © 1982 by Thomas Nelson, Inc. Used by permission.

Scripture quotations marked (TLB) are taken from The Holy Bible, The Living Bible
Translation, Copyright © 1971. Used by permission of Tyndale House Publishers,
Incorporated, Wheaton, Illinois 60189. All rights reserved.

Scripture quotations marked (NLT) are taken from The Holy Bible, New Living
Translation, Copyright © 1996. Used by permission of Tyndale House Publishers,
Incorporated, Wheaton, Illinois 60189. All rights reserved.

Printed in the United States of America
Cover Design: Nick Long
Page Layout: Bart Dawson

1 2 3 4 5 6 7 8 9 10 • 03 04 05 06 07 08 09 10

For Friends Everywhere

Table of Contents

Introduction

◈

In your hands, you hold a book entitled *Promises, Praises, and Prayers for Friends*. Perhaps you received this book as a gift from a trusted friend, or perhaps you picked it up on your own. Either way, you will be blessed *if* you take the words of these pages to heart.

This text addresses topics of interest to Christians of all ages. Each brief chapter contains Bible verses, quotations (from noted pastors, scholars, and hymnists), and a prayer. The ideas in each chapter are intended as powerful reminders of God's commandments and of the joys of Christian friendship.

Genuine, lifelong friendship is ordained by God. As such, it should be valued and nurtured. As Christians, we are commanded to love one another, and the familiar words of 1st Corinthians 13:13 remind us that love and charity are among God's greatest gifts: *But now faith, hope, love, abide these three; but the greatest of these is love (NASB).*

Friendship is a glorious gift, praised by God. Let us praise Him for that gift by making it grow.

Abundance

...these things I speak in the world, that they might have my joy fulfilled in themselves.

John 17:13 KJV

...I am come that they might have life, and that they might have it more abundantly.

John 10:10 KJV

Commit to the Lord whatever you do, and your plans will succeed.

Proverbs 16:3 NIV

But as for you, be strong and do not give up, for your work will be rewarded.

II Chronicles 15:7 NIV

His lord said unto him, Well done, thou good and faithful servant: thou hast been faithful over a few things, I will make thee ruler over many things: enter thou into the joy of thy lord.

Matthew 25:21 KJV

LET US PRAISE GOD FOR HIS ABUNDANCE.

Jesus intended for us to be overwhelmed by the blessings of regular days. He said it was the reason he had come: "I am come that they might have life, and that they might have it more abundantly."

Gloria Gaither

We honor God by asking for great things when they are a part of His promise. We dishonor Him and cheat ourselves when we ask for molehills where He has promised mountains.

Vance Havner

Dear Heavenly Father,

You have promised an abundant life for me through Your Son, Jesus. Thank You, Lord, for Your abundance. Guide me according to Your will, so that I might be a worthy servant to You and a worthy friend to those who cross my path, this day and every day.

Amen

Accepting Christ

And we have seen and testify that the Father has sent his Son to be the Savior of the world.

1 John 4:14 NIV

Blessed be the God and Father of our Lord Jesus Christ, who according to His great mercy has caused us to be born again to a living hope through the resurrection of Jesus Christ from the dead.

1 Peter 1:3 NASB

For the wages of sin is death, but the gift of God is eternal life in Christ Jesus our Lord.

Romans 6:23 NIV

For God so loved the world, that he gave his only begotten Son, that whosoever believeth in him should not perish, but have everlasting life.

John 3:16 KJV

LET US PRAISE GOD BY ACCEPTING HIS SON.

Come into my heart, Lord Jesus; come into today, come into stay, come into my heart, Lord Jesus.

Harry D. Clarke

When once you get into personal contact with Jesus Christ, you will never be the same again.

Oswald Chambers

Ask Christ to come into your heart to forgive you and help you. When you do, Christ will take up residence in your life by His Holy Spirit, and when you face temptations and trials, you will no longer face them alone.

Billy Graham

Dear Heavenly Father,

You gave Your Son that I might have life eternal. Thank You for this priceless gift and for the joy I feel in my heart when I give You my thoughts, my prayers, my praise, and my life.

Amen

Adversity

For whatsoever is born of God overcometh the world....

I John 5:4 KJV

Come to me, all you who are weary and burdened, and I will give you rest. Take my yoke upon you and learn from me, for I am gentle and humble in heart, and you will find rest for your souls. For my yoke is easy and my burden is light.

Matthew 11:28-30 NIV

God is our refuge and strength, always ready to help in times of trouble. So we will not fear, even if earthquakes come and mountains crumble to the sea.

Psalm 46:1-2 NTL

In my distress I called to the Lord; I called out to my God. From his temple he heard my voice; my cry came to his ears.

2 Samuel 22:7 NIV

LET US PRAISE GOD WHEN HE PROTECTS US IN TIMES OF ADVERSITY.

How sweet the name of Jesus sounds in a believer's ear! It soothes his sorrows, heals his wounds, and drives away his fear.

John Newton

I have a great need for Christ; I have a great Christ for my need.

C. H. Spurgeon

No time is too hard for God; no situation is too difficult.

Norman Vincent Peale

Dear Heavenly Father,

You are my strength in times of adversity. When I am troubled, You comfort me. When I am discouraged, You lift me up. Whatever my circumstances, Lord, let me trust Your plan for my life. And, when my family and friends are troubled, let me remind them of Your love, Your wisdom, and Your grace.

Amen

The Bible

There's nothing like the written Word of God for showing you the way to salvation through faith in Christ Jesus. Every part of Scripture is God-breathed and useful one way or another, showing us truth, exposing our rebellion, correcting our mistakes, training us to live God's way. Through the Word we are put together and shaped up for the tasks God has for us.

2 Timothy 3:15-17 MSG

For the word of God is quick, and powerful, and sharper than any two-edged sword, piercing even to the dividing asunder of soul and spirit, and of the joints and marrow, and is a discerner of the thoughts and intents of the heart.

Hebrews 4:12 KJV

You will be a good servant of Christ Jesus, constantly nourished on the words of the faith and of the sound doctrine which you have been following.

1 Timothy 4:6 NASB

LET US PRAISE GOD FOR HIS HOLY WORD.

Holy Bible, book divine, precious treasure, thou art mine; mine to tell me whence I came; mine to teach me what I am.

John Burton

In reading the Bible, we study to know God, to hear his voice, and to be changed by him as we grow in holiness.

James Montgomery Boice

Dear Heavenly Father,

The Bible is Your gift to me; let me use it. When I stray from Your Holy Word, Lord, I suffer. But, when I place Your Word at the very center of my life, I am blessed. Make me a faithful student of Your Word so that I might be a faithful servant in Your world, this day and every day.

Amen

Cheerfulness

A cheerful look brings joy to the heart, and good news gives health to the bones.

Proverbs 15:30 NIV

Delight thyself also in the LORD; and he shall give thee the desires of thine heart.

Psalm 37:4 KJV

So now we can rejoice in our wonderful new relationship with God—all because of what our Lord Jesus Christ has done for us in making us friends of God.

Romans 5:11 NLT

Be cheerful no matter what; pray all the time; thank God no matter what happens. This is the way God wants you who belong to Christ Jesus to live.

1 Thessalonians 5:16-18 MSG

LET US PRAISE GOD CHEERFULLY.

When I think of God, my heart is so full of joy that the notes leap and dance as they leave my pen; and since God has given me a cheerful heart, I serve him with a cheerful spirit.

Franz Joseph Haydn

Cheerfulness is no sin, nor is there any grace in a solemn cast of countenance.

John Newton

Dear Heavenly Father,

You have blessed me beyond measure; let me praise You joyfully. Make me be a cheerful Christian, Lord. Keep me always mindful of Your gifts, and let me share Your joy with my family, with my friends, and with all who cross my path this day and every day.

Amen

Contentment

Let your conduct be without covetousness; be content with such things as you have. For He Himself has said, "I will never leave you nor forsake you."

Hebrews 13:5 NKJV

I have learned, in whatsoever state I am, therewith to be content.

Philippians 4:11 KJV

A heart at peace gives life to the body, but envy rots the bones.

Proverbs 14:30 NIV

I know what it is to be in need, and I know what it is to have plenty. I have learned the secret of being content in any and every situation, whether well fed or hungry, whether living in plenty or in want. I can do everything through him who gives me strength.

Philippians 4:12-13 NIV

LET US PRAISE GOD AND BE CONTENTED.

If we know we have pleased God, contentment will be our consolation, for what pleases God will please us.

Kay Arthur

Next to faith this is the highest art: to be content with the calling in which God has placed you. I have not learned it yet.

Martin Luther

Dear Heavenly Father,

You are my contentment and my peace. I find protection when I seek Your healing hand. Let me look to You, Lord, for the peace You have offered me through the gift of Your Son, and let me share His peace with my friends and my family, this day and every day.

Amen

Conversion

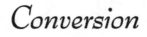

Therefore, if anyone is in Christ, he is a new creation; the old has gone, the new has come!

2 Corinthians 5:17 NIV

Jesus answered and said unto him, Verily, verily, I say unto thee, Except a man be born again, he cannot see the kingdom of God.

John 3:3 KJV

And Jesus called a little child unto him, and set him in the midst of them, and said, Verily I say unto you, Except ye be converted, and become as little children, ye shall not enter into the kingdom of heaven.

Matthew 18:2-3 KJV

LET US PRAISE GOD FOR CHANGING OUR LIVES.

———————◈———————

Since He looked upon me my heart is not my own. He hath run away to heaven with it.

Samuel Rutherford

We cannot change our hearts, but we can change our minds; and when we change our minds, God will change our hearts.

Vance Havner

The salvation of Jesus Christ enables a man to see for the first time in his life.

Oswald Chambers

Dear Heavenly Father,

When I accepted Jesus as my personal savior, You changed me forever and made me whole. Let me share Your Son's message with my friends, with my family, and with the world. You are a God of love, redemption, conversion, and salvation. Let me praise you today and forever.

Amen

Courage

Be strong and courageous, and do the work. Do not be afraid or discouraged, for the Lord God, my God, is with you.

1 Chronicles 28:20 NIV

For God hath not given us the spirit of fear; but of power, and of love, and of a sound mind.

2 Timothy 1:7 KJV

The LORD himself goes before you and will be with you; he will never leave you nor forsake you. Do not be afraid; do not be discouraged.

Deuteronomy 31:8 NIV

Do not be afraid...I am your shield, your very great reward.

Genesis 15:1 NIV

Fear of man will prove to be a snare, but whoever trusts in the LORD is kept safe.

Proverbs 29:25 NIV

LET US PRAISE GOD FOR THE GIFT OF COURAGE.

God of grace and God of glory, on Thy people pour Thy power. Grant us wisdom; grant us courage for the facing of this hour.

Harry Emerson Fosdick

Courage is contagious.

Billy Graham

Take courage. We walk in the wilderness today and in the Promised Land tomorrow.

D. L. Moody

Dear Heavenly Father,

Sometimes, this world is a fearful place. Yet, You have promised me that You are with me always. With You as my protector, I am not afraid. Today, Dear Lord, I will live courageously as I place my trust in Your everlasting power and my faith in Your everlasting love.

Amen

Encouragement

Do not let any unwholesome talk come out of your mouths, but only what is helpful for building others up according to their needs, that it may benefit those who listen.

Ephesians 4:29 NIV

Let us consider how to stimulate one another to love and good deeds.

Hebrews 10:24 NASB

Let the word of Christ dwell in you richly in all wisdom; teaching and admonishing one another in psalms and hymns and spiritual songs, singing with grace in your hearts to the Lord.

Colossians 3:16 KJV

A cheerful look brings joy to the heart, and good news gives health to the bones.

Proverbs 15:30 NIV

LET US PRAISE GOD FOR ENCOURAGING FRIENDS.

There are no words to express the abyss between isolation and having one ally.

G. K. Chesterton

No journey is complete that does not lead through some dark valleys. We can properly comfort others only with the comfort we ourselves have been given by God.

Vance Havner

He climbs highest who helps another up.

Zig Ziglar

Dear Heavenly Father,

Make me sensitive to the many gifts of encouragement I receive each day. And, let me be a source of encouragement to all who cross my path. The Bible tells of Your servant Barnabas. Like Barnabas, I, too, want to be an encourager to my family and friends so that I might do Your work and share Your love.

Amen

Eternal Life

◈

But now being made free from sin, and become servants to God, ye have your fruit unto holiness, and the end everlasting life. For the wages of sin is death; but the gift of God is eternal life through Jesus Christ our Lord.

Romans 6:22-23 KJV

Verily, verily, I say unto you, He that heareth my word, and believeth on him that sent me, hath everlasting life, and shall not come into condemnation; but is passed from death unto life.

John 5:24 KJV

He that loveth his life shall lose it; and he that hateth his life in this world shall keep it unto life eternal.

John 12:25 KJV

For if ye live after the flesh, ye shall die: but if ye through the Spirit do mortify the deeds of the body, ye shall live.

Romans 8:13 KJV

LET US PRAISE GOD FOR THE GIFT OF ETERNAL LIFE.

If you are a believer, your judgment will not determine your eternal destiny. Christ's finished work on Calvary was applied to you the moment you accepted Christ as Savior.

Beth Moore

Christ is the only liberator whose liberation lasts forever.

Malcolm Muggeridge

Dear Heavenly Father,

I know that this world is not my home; I am only here for a brief while. And, You have given me the priceless gift of eternal life through Your Son Jesus. Keep the hope of heaven fresh in my heart, and, while I am in this world, help me to pass through it with faith in my heart and praise on my lips . . . for You.

Amen

Evil

———◆———

Do not ye yet understand, that whatsoever entereth in at the mouth goeth into the belly, and is cast out into the draught? But those things which proceed out of the mouth come forth from the heart; and they defile the man. For out of the heart proceed evil thoughts, murders, adulteries, fornications, thefts, false witness, blasphemies: these are the things which defile a man: but to eat with unwashen hands defileth not a man.

Matthew 15:17-20 KJV

I will set no wicked thing before mine eyes....

Psalm 101:3 KJV

A fool finds pleasure in evil conduct, but a man of understanding delights in wisdom.

Proverbs 10:23 NIV

Be not overcome of evil, but overcome evil with good.

Romans 12:21 KJV

LET US PRAISE GOD FOR HIS PROTECTION FROM EVIL.

God shapes the world by prayer. The more praying there is in the world, the better the world will be, and the mightier will be the forces against evil.

E. M. Bounds

Of two evils, choose neither.

C. H. Spurgeon

The only thing necessary for the triumph of evil is for good men to do nothing.

Edmund Burke

Dear Heavenly Father,

Because You have given Your children free will, the world is a place where evil threatens our lives and our souls. Protect us, Father, from the evils and temptations of this difficult age. Help us to trust You, Father, and to obey Your Word, knowing that Your ultimate victory over evil is both inevitable and complete.

Amen

Example

Your attitude should be the same as that of Christ Jesus: Who, being in very nature God, did not consider equality with God something to be grasped, but made himself nothing, taking the very nature of a servant, being made in human likeness. And being found in appearance as a man, he humbled himself and became obedient to death— even death on a cross!

Philippians 2:5-8 NIV

Make the Master proud of you by being good citizens. Respect the authorities, whatever their level; they are God's emissaries for keeping order.

I Peter 2:13-14 MSG

Be thou an example of the believers, in word, in conversation, in charity, in spirit, in faith, in purity.

I Timothy 4:12 KJV

LET US PRAISE GOD BY THE EXAMPLES WE SET FOR OTHERS.

If we have the true love of God in our hearts, we will show it in our lives. We will not have to go up and down the earth proclaiming it. We will show it in everything we say or do.

D. L. Moody

I'd rather see a sermon than hear one any day; I'd rather one should walk with me than merely tell the way.

Edgar A. Guest

Of all commentaries on the Scriptures, good examples are the best.

John Donne

Dear Heavenly Father,

Make me a worthy example to my family and friends. And, let my words and my deeds serve as a testimony to the changes You have made in my life. Let me praise You, Father, by following in the footsteps of Your Son, and let others see Him through me.

Amen

Faith

Have faith in the LORD your God and you will be upheld; have faith in his prophets and you will be successful.

2 Chronicles 20:20 NIV

If you do not stand firm in your faith, you will not stand at all.

Isaiah 7:9 NIV

I tell you the truth, if you have faith as small as a mustard seed, you can say to this mountain, "Move from here to there" and it will move. Nothing will be impossible for you.

Matthew 17:20 NIV

Through faith we understand that the worlds were framed by the word of God, so that things which are seen were not made of things which do appear.

Hebrews 11:3 KJV

LET US PRAISE GOD BY LIVING FAITHFULLY.

At the cross, where I first saw the light, and the burden of my heart rolled away. It was there by faith I received my sight.

Ralph E. Hudson

A faith that hasn't been tested can't be trusted.

Adrian Rogers

Faith is like an empty, open hand stretched out towards God, with nothing to offer and everything to receive.

John Calvin

Dear Heavenly Father,

I want to be Your faithful servant. Guide my thoughts, my words, and my actions. Let me live each day with an unshakable faith in You, Father, trusting You in every circumstance. And, let me be an example of faithful living to my friends and family so that I might be a worthy ambassador for You.

Amen

Forgiveness

You have heard that it was said, "Love your neighbor and hate your enemy." But I tell you: Love your enemies and pray for those who persecute you.

Matthew 5:43-44 NIV

Hatred stirs up dissension, but love covers over all wrongs.

Proverbs 10:12 NIV

Above all, love each other deeply, because love covers a multitude of sins.

I Peter 4:8 NIV

And be ye kind one to another, tenderhearted, forgiving one another, even as God for Christ's sake hath forgiven you.

Ephesians 4:32 KJV

LET US PRAISE GOD BY FORGIVING OTHERS.

I believe that forgiveness can become a continuing cycle: because God forgives us, we're able to forgive others; because we forgive others, God forgives us. Scripture presents both parts of the circle.

Shirley Dobson

The only true forgiveness is that which is offered and extended even before the offender has apologized and sought it.

Søren Kierkegaard

Dear Heavenly Father,

Forgiveness is Your commandment, and I know that I should forgive others just as You have forgiven me. But, genuine forgiveness is difficult. Help me to forgive those who have injured me, and deliver me from the traps of anger and bitterness. Forgiveness is Your way, Lord; let it be mine.

Amen

Friendship

You are my friends if you do what I command. I no longer call you servants, because a servant does not know his master's business. Instead, I have called you friends, for everything that I learned from my Father I have made known to you.

John 15:14-15 NIV

A friend loves at all times, and a brother is born for adversity.

Proverbs 17:17 NIV

How good and pleasant it is when brothers live together in unity!

Psalm 133:1 NIV

Iron sharpeneth iron; so a man sharpeneth the countenance of his friend.

Proverbs 27:17 KJV

LET US PRAISE GOD FOR THE GIFT OF FRIENDSHIP.

Some people come into our lives and quickly go. Some people stay for awhile and leave footprints on our hearts, and we are never the same.

Anonymous

In friendship, God opens your eyes to the glories of Himself.

Joni Eareckson Tada

A true friend is the gift of God, and only he who made hearts can unite them.

Robert South

Dear Heavenly Father,

You seek abundance and joy for me and for all Your children. I praise You for the gift of friendship. Help me to be a loyal friend, Lord. Let me be ready to listen, ready to encourage, and ready to offer a helping hand. Let me be a worthy servant to You, Lord, and a worthy friend. And, let the love of Jesus shine through me today and forever.

Amen

47

Generosity

Let us not lose heart in doing good, for in due time we shall reap if we do not grow weary. So then, while we have opportunity, let us do good to all men, and especially to those who are of the household of the faith.

Galatians 6:9-10 NASB

Who is wise and understanding among you? Let him show it by his good life, by deeds done in the humility that comes from wisdom.

James 3:13 NIV

Freely you have received, freely give.

Matthew 10:8 NIV

He that hath two coats, let him impart to him that hath none; and he that hath meat, let him do likewise.

Luke 3:11 KJV

LET US PRAISE GOD BY GIVING GENEROUSLY TO OTHERS.

———————◈———————

I expect to pass through this life but once. If, therefore, there be any good thing I can do to any fellow being, let me do it now, and not defer or neglect it, as I shall not pass this way again.

William Penn

We are never more like God than when we give.

Chuck Swindoll

It is the duty of every Christian to be Christ to his neighbor.

Martin Luther

Dear Heavenly Father,

You have been so generous with me; let me be generous with others. Help me to give generously of my time and my possessions as I care for my family, for my friends, and for those in need. And, make me a humble giver, Lord, so that all the glory and the praise might be Yours alone.

Amen

Gifts

Since we have gifts that differ according to the grace given to us, let each exercise them accordingly: if prophecy, according to the proportion of his faith; if service, in his serving; or he who teaches, in his teaching; or he who exhorts, in his exhortation; he who gives, with liberality; he who leads, with diligence; he who shows mercy, with cheerfulness.

Romans 12:6-8 NASB

Do not neglect the spiritual gift that is within you....

I Timothy 4:14 NASB

Now there are diversities of gifts, but the same Spirit.

I Corinthians 12:4 KJV

Every good gift and every perfect gift is from above, and cometh down from the Father of lights.

James 1:17 KJV

LET US PRAISE GOD FOR HIS GIFTS.

God is still in the process of dispensing gifts, and He uses ordinary individuals like us to develop those gifts in other people.

Howard Hendricks

The Lord has abundantly blessed me all of my life. I'm not trying to pay Him back for all of His wonderful gifts; I just realize that He gave them to me to give away.

Lisa Whelchel

Dear Heavenly Father,

I praise You for Your priceless gifts. I give thanks for Your creation, for Your Son, and for the unique talents and opportunities that You have given me. Let me use my gifts for the glory of Your kingdom, this day and every day.

Amen

God's Creation

For every house is built by someone, but the builder of all things is God.

Hebrews 3:4 NASB

Know that the Lord Himself is God; It is He who has made us, and not we ourselves; We are His people and the sheep of His pasture.

Psalm 100:3 NASB

Thou, Lord, in the beginning hast laid the foundation of the earth; and the heavens are the works of thine hands.

Hebrews 1:10 KJV

And to every beast of the earth and to every bird of the sky and to every thing that moves on the earth which has life . . . God saw all that He had made, and behold, it was very good.

Genesis 1:30-31 NASB

LET US PRAISE GOD FOR HIS MARVELOUS CREATION.

───────◆───────

Today, you will encounter God's creation. When you see the beauty around you, let each detail remind you to lift your head in praise.

Max Lucado

I love to think of nature as an unlimited broadcasting station through which God speaks to us every hour—if we will only tune in.

George Washington Carver

Dear Heavenly Father,

You have created a universe that is glorious to behold yet impossible to comprehend. I praise You for Your creation, Father, and for the sense of awe and wonder that You have placed in my heart. This is the day that You have made; let me use it according to Your will and in the service of Your Son.

Amen

God's Discipline

No discipline seems pleasant at the time, but painful. Later on, however, it produces a harvest of righteousness and peace for those who have been trained by it.

Hebrews 12:11 NIV

For the wrath of God is revealed from heaven against all ungodliness and unrighteousness of men....

Romans 1:18 KJV

My son, despise not the chastening of the LORD; Neither be weary of his correction for whom the LORD loveth he correcteth....

Proverbs 3:11-12 KJV

My son, do not make light of the Lord's discipline, and do not lose heart when he rebukes you, because the Lord disciplines those he loves....

Hebrews 12:5 NIV

LET US PRAISE GOD FOR HIS DISCIPLINE.

God's actual divine essence and his will are absolutely beyond all human thought, human understanding or wisdom; in short, they are and ever will be incomprehensible, inscrutable, and altogether hidden to human reason.

Martin Luther

Only grief and disappointment can result from continued violation of the divine principles that underlie the spiritual life.

A. W. Tozer

Dear Heavenly Father,

When I stray from Your commandments, You offer me Your discipline and Your love. When I am wrong, You correct me in Your own way and in Your own time. I praise You for Your discipline, Father. Let me grow in the wisdom of Your ways, and let me live in accordance with Your will.

Amen

God's Faithfulness

Blessed is he whose help is the God of Jacob, whose hope is in the LORD his God, the Maker of heaven and earth, the sea, and everything in them—the LORD, who remains faithful forever.

Psalm 146:5-6 NIV

Because of the LORD'S great love we are not consumed, for his compassions never fail. They are new every morning; great is your faithfulness.

Lamentations 3:22-23 NIV

For the Lord is good. His unfailing love continues forever, and his faithfulness continues to each generation.

Psalm 100:5 NLT

I will sing of the tender mercies of the Lord forever! Young and old will hear of your faithfulness. Your unfailing love will last forever. Your faithfulness is as enduring as the heavens.

Psalm 89:1-2 NLT

LET US PRAISE GOD FOR HIS FAITHFULNESS.

———————◆———————

God's faithfulness has never depended on the faithfulness of his children.... God is greater than our weakness. In fact, I think, it is our weakness that reveals how great God is.

Max Lucado

No matter what we are going through, no matter how long the waiting for answers, of one thing we may be sure. God is faithful. He keeps His promises. What He starts, He finishes...including His perfect work in us.

Gloria Gaither

Dear Heavenly Father,

Your faithfulness is everlasting. You are faithful to me even when I am not faithful to You. Today, let me serve You with all my heart, my soul, and my mind. And then, let me rest in the knowledge of Your unchanging and constant love for me.

Amen

God's Laws

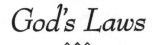

Blessed are they whose ways are blameless, who walk according to the law of the Lord. Blessed are they who keep his statutes and who seek him with all their heart.

Psalm 119:1-2 NIV

Jesus said unto him, Thou shalt love the Lord thy God with all thy heart, and with all thy soul, and with all thy mind. This is the first and great commandment. And the second is like unto it, Thou shalt love thy neighbor as thyself. On these two commandments hang all the law and the prophets.

Matthew 22:37-40 KJV

Whosoever transgresseth, and abideth not in the doctrine of Christ, hath not God. He that abideth in the doctrine of Christ, he hath both the Father and the Son.

2 John 9 KJV

LET US PRAISE GOD FOR HIS LAWS.

———————◈———————

Faith reposes on the character of God, and if we believe that God is perfect, we must conclude that his ways are perfect also.

A. W. Tozer

We learn his truth by obeying it.

Oswald Chambers

God's word is not obsolete; it is absolute.

Vance Havner

Dear Heavenly Father,

Your laws are everlasting and unchanging. When I follow Your commandments, I am blessed. Today, let me study Your Word and discover Your will for my life. Your laws are perfect, Lord; let me honor You by obeying them.

Amen

God's Love

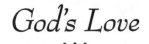

The Lord is kind and merciful, slow to get angry, full of unfailing love. The Lord is good to everyone. He showers compassion on all his creation.

Psalm 145:8-9 NLT

O God, you are my God, earnestly I seek you; my soul thirsts for you, my body longs for you, in a dry and weary land where there is no water. I have seen you in the sanctuary and beheld your power and your glory. Because your love is better than life, my lips will glorify you.

Psalm 63:1-3 NIV

The unfailing love of the Lord never ends!

Lamentations 3:22 NLT

You are my God, and I will give you thanks; you are my God, and I will exalt you. Give thanks to the LORD, for he is good; his love endures forever.

Psalm 118:28-29 NIV

LET US PRAISE GOD FOR HIS LOVE.

———◈———

Jesus loves me! This I know, for the Bible tells me so. Little ones to Him belong; they are weak, but He is strong.

Anna B. Warner

The essence of God's being is love—He never separates Himself from that.

Kay Arthur

God loves us the way we are, but He loves us too much to leave us that way.

Leighton Ford

Dear Heavenly Father,

You are love. I love You, Lord, and as I love You more, I am able to love my family and friends more. Let me be Your loving servant, Heavenly Father, today and throughout eternity.

Amen

God's Mercy

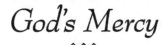

He has shown you, O man, what is good; And what does the LORD require of you but to do justly, to love mercy, and to walk humbly with your God?

Micah 6:8 NKJV

But in your great mercy you did not put an end to them or abandon them, for you are a gracious and merciful God.

Nehemiah 9:31 NIV

But the mercy of the LORD is from everlasting to everlasting upon them that fear him, and his righteousness unto children's children....

Psalm 103:17 KJV

But when the kindness and love of God our Savior appeared, he saved us, not because of righteous things we had done, but because of his mercy.

Titus 3:4-5 NIV

LET US PRAISE GOD FOR HIS MERCY

God's heart of mercy provides for us not only pardon from sin but also a daily provision of spiritual food to strengthen us.

Jim Cymbala

No matter what we've been, when we are touched by God, we can honestly say, "Now I'm no longer the same!"

Gloria Gaither

There's a wideness in God's mercy like the wideness of the sea; there's a kindness in His justice which is more than liberty.

Frederick W. Faber

Dear Heavenly Father,

You have blessed me with so much: Your love, Your mercy, and Your grace. Enable me to be merciful toward others, Father, just as You have been merciful toward me so that I might share Your love with all who cross my path.

Amen

God's Plan

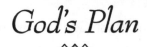

To every thing there is a season, and a time to every purpose under the heaven.

Ecclesiastes 3:1 KJV

It is God who works in you to will and to act according to his good purpose.

Philippians 2:13 NIV

In his heart a man plans his course, but the Lord determines his steps.

Proverbs 16:9 NIV

And we know that in all things God works for the good of those who love him, who have been called according to his purpose.

Romans 8:28 NIV

The Lord will work out his plans for my life— for your faithful love, O Lord, endures forever.

Psalm 138:8 NLT

LET US PRAISE GOD FOR THE WISDOM OF HIS DIVINE PLAN.

When God is involved, anything can happen. Be open and stay that way. God has a beautiful way of bringing good vibrations out of broken chords.

Chuck Swindoll

The Almighty does nothing without reason, although the frail mind of man cannot explain the reason.

Saint Augustine

I'm convinced that there is nothing that can happen to me in this life that is not precisely designed by a sovereign Lord to give me the opportunity to learn to know Him.

Elisabeth Elliot

Dear Heavenly Father,

You have a plan for my life. Let me discover it and live it. Today, I will seek Your will, knowing that when I trust in You, dear Father, I am eternally blessed.

Amen

God's Provision for
Our Needs

And we desire that each one of you show the same diligence so as to realize the full assurance of hope until the end, so that you will not be sluggish, but imitators of those who through faith and patience inherit the promises.

Hebrews 6:11-12 NASB

The Lord protects the simplehearted; when I was in great need, he saved me.

Psalm 116:6 NIV

If God be for us, who can be against us?

Romans 8:31 KJV

For you have need of endurance, so that when you have done the will of God, you may receive what was promised.

Hebrews 10:36 NASB

LET US PRAISE GOD BECAUSE HE PROVIDES FOR OUR NEEDS.

We shall find in Christ enough of everything we need—for the body, for the mind, and for the spirit—to do what He wants us to do as long as He wants us to do it.

Vance Havner

God's gifts put man's best dreams to shame.

Elisabeth Barrett Browning

Dear Heavenly Father,

You have promised that You will provide for my needs, and I trust that promise. But sometimes, because of my imperfect faith, I fall prey to worry and doubt. Today, give me the courage to trust You completely. You are my protector, dear Lord; let me praise You, let me love You, and let me trust in the perfect wisdom of Your plan.

Amen

God's Support

I am holding you by your right hand—I, the LORD your God. And I say to you, "Do not be afraid. I am here to help you...."

Isaiah 41:13 NLT

"Lord Help!" they cried in their trouble, and he saved them from their distress.

Psalm 107:28 NLT

The Lord is my rock, my fortress and my savior; my God is my rock in whom I find protection. He is my shield, the strength of my salvation, and my stronghold.

Psalm 18:2 NLT

For the eyes of the Lord range throughout the earth to strengthen those whose hearts are fully committed to him.

2 Chronicles 16:9 NIV

LET US PRAISE GOD FOR HIS CARE AND PROTECTION.

———————◇———————

Thou art my Counselor, my Pattern, and my Guide, and Thou my Shepherd art.

Issac Watts

God is the light in my darkness, the voice in my silence.

Helen Keller

Faith is not merely your holding on to God—it is God holding on to you.

E. Stanley Jones

Dear Heavenly Father,

You never leave or forsake me. You are always with me, protecting me and encouraging me. Whatever this day may bring, I thank You for Your love and Your strength. Let me lean upon You, Father, this day and forever.

Amen

God's Timing

He has made everything beautiful in its time. He has also set eternity in the hearts of men; yet they cannot fathom what God has done from beginning to end.

Ecclesiastes 3:11 NIV

Wait patiently on the Lord. Be brave and courageous. Yes, wait patiently on the Lord.

Psalm 27:14 NLT

Humble yourselves therefore under the mighty hand of God, that he may exalt you in due time.

1 Peter 5:6 KJV

I wait quietly before God, for my salvation comes from him. He alone is my rock and my salvation, my fortress where I will never be shaken.

Psalm 62:1-2 NLT

LET US PRAISE GOD FOR HIS PERFECT TIMING.

The Lord may not come when you want him, but he's always going to be there on time.

Lou Gossett, Jr.

God has a designated time when his promise will be fulfilled and the prayer will be answered.

Jim Cymbala

We forget that God sometimes has to say "No." We pray to Him as our heavenly Father, and like wise human fathers, He often says, "No," not from whim or caprice, but from wisdom, from love, and from knowing what is best for us.

Peter Marshall

Dear Heavenly Father,

Your timing is seldom my timing, but Your timing is always right for me. You are my Father, and You have a plan for my life that is grander than I can imagine. When I am impatient, remind me that You are never early or late. You are always on time, Lord, so let me trust in You . . . always.

Amen

Golden Rule

See that no one pays back evil for evil, but always try to do good to each other and to everyone else.

1 Thessalonians 5:15 TLB

Do to others as you would have them do to you.

Luke 6:31 NIV

Each of you should look not only to your own interests, but also to the interest of others.

Philippians 2:4 NIV

Judge not, and ye shall not be judged: condemn not, and ye shall not be condemned: forgive, and ye shall be forgiven: give, and it shall be given unto you.... For with the same measure that ye mete withal it shall be measured to you again.

Luke 6:37-38 KJV

LET US PRAISE GOD FOR FRIENDS WHO PRACTICE THE GOLDEN RULE.

We should behave to our friends as we would wish our friends to behave to us.

Aristotle

Employ whatever God has entrusted you with, in doing good, all possible good, in every possible kind and degree.

John Wesley

Goodness is the only investment that never fails.

Henry David Thoreau

Dear Heavenly Father,

I thank You for friends and family members who practice the Golden Rule. Because I expect to be treated with kindness, let me be kind. Because I wish to be loved, let me be loving. Because I need forgiveness, let me be merciful. In all things, Lord, let me live by the Golden Rule, and let me express my gratitude to those who offer kindness and generosity to me.

Amen

Grace

And the God of all grace, who called you to his eternal glory in Christ, after you have suffered a little while, will himself restore you and make you strong, firm and steadfast.

1 Peter 5:10 NIV

For by grace are ye saved through faith; and that not of yourselves: it is the gift of God: not of works, lest any man should boast.

Ephesians 2:8-9 KJV

But grow in grace, and in the knowledge of our Lord and Saviour Jesus Christ....

2 Peter 3:18 KJV

For all have sinned and fall short of the glory of God, and are justified freely by his grace through the redemption that came by Christ Jesus.

Romans 3:23-24 NIV

LET US PRAISE GOD FOR HIS GRACE.

Marvelous, infinite, matchless grace, freely bestowed on all who believe! God's Grace that will pardon and cleanse within!

Julia H. Johnston

Grace is God's free, spontaneous, unsolicited, even unreturned love, which finds its origin in itself, not in its object.

John Stott

The will of God will never lead you where the grace of God cannot keep you.

Warren Wiersbe

Dear Heavenly Father,

Accepting Your grace can be hard. Somehow, I feel that I must earn Your love and Your acceptance. Yet, the Bible promises that You love me and save me by Your grace. It is a gift I can only accept and cannot earn. Thank You for Your priceless, everlasting gift.

Amen

Gratitude

Be cheerful no matter what; pray all the time; thank God no matter what happens. This is the way God wants you who belong to Christ Jesus to live.

1 Thessalonians 5:16-18 MSG

Everything created by God is good, and nothing is to be rejected, if it is received with gratitude; for it is sanctified by means of the word of God and prayer.

1 Timothy 4:4-5 NASB

Surely the righteous shall give thanks unto thy name: the upright shall dwell in thy presence.

Psalm 140:13 KJV

Therefore, since we receive a kingdom which cannot be shaken, let us show gratitude, by which we may offer to God an acceptable service with reverence and awe....

Hebrews 12:28 NASB

LET US PRAISE GOD WITH GRATEFUL HEARTS.

It is only with gratitude that life becomes rich.

Dietrich Bonhoeffer

Give thanks with a grateful heart; give thanks to the Holy One; give thanks because He's given Jesus Christ, His Son.

Henry Smith

We should spend as much time in thanking God for his benefits as we do asking him for them.

St. Vincent de Paul

Dear Heavenly Father,

Let my attitude be one of gratitude. You have given me much; when I think of Your grace and goodness, I am humbled and thankful. Today, let me express my thanksgiving, Father, not just through my words but also through my deeds . . . and may all the glory be Yours.

Amen

Grief

I have heard your prayer and seen your tears; I will heal you....

2 Kings 20:5 NIV

The Lord shall give thee rest from thy sorrow, and from thy fear....

Isaiah 14:3 KJV

Blessed are those who mourn, for they will be comforted.

Matthew 5:4 NIV

When I sit in darkness, the Lord shall be a light unto me.

Micah 7:8 KJV

I cried out to the Lord in my suffering, and he heard me. He set me free from all my fears.

Psalm 34:6 NLT

LET US PRAISE GOD EVEN IN TIMES OF SORROW.

There is no pit so deep that God's love is not deeper still.

Corrie ten Boom

You who suffer take heart. Christ is the answer to sorrow.

Billy Graham

God whispers to us in our pleasures, speaks in our conscience, but shouts in our pain.

C. S. Lewis

Dear Heavenly Father,

You have promised that You will not give us more than we can bear; You have promised to lift us out of our grief and despair; You have promised to put a new song on our lips. Today, Lord, I pray for those who mourn, and I thank You for sustaining all of us in our days of sorrow. May we trust You always and praise You forever.

Amen

Happiness

I've learned by now to be quite content whatever my circumstances. I'm just as happy with little as with much, with much as with little. I've found the recipe for being happy whether full or hungry, hands full or hands empty.

Philippians 4:11-12 MSG

Happy is he...whose hope is in the LORD his God.

Psalm 146:5 KJV

Happy is the man that findeth wisdom, and the man that getteth understanding.

Proverbs 3:13 KJV

Delight thyself also in the LORD; and he shall give thee the desires of thine heart.

Psalm 37:4 KJV

LET US PRAISE GOD WITH HAPPINESS IN OUR HEARTS.

———————◆———————

The happiest people in the world are not those who have no problems, but the people who have learned to live with those things that are less than perfect.

James Dobson

Our thoughts, not our circumstances, determine our happiness.

John Maxwell

Make God's will the focus of your life day by day. If you seek to please Him and Him alone, you'll find yourself satisfied with life.

Kay Arthur

Dear Heavenly Father,

You are my strength and my joy. I will rejoice in the day that You have made, and I will give thanks for the countless blessings that You have given me. Let me be a joyful Christian, Father, as I share Your Good News with friends, with family, and with the world.

Amen

Honesty

The man of integrity walks securely, but he who takes crooked paths will be found out.

Proverbs 10:9 NIV

Therefore, seeing we have this ministry, as we have received mercy, we faint not; but have renounced the hidden things of dishonesty, not walking in craftiness, nor handling the word of God deceitfully; but, by manifestation of the truth, commending ourselves to every man's conscience in the sight of God.

2 Corinthians 4:1-2 KJV

A false balance is abomination to the LORD: but a just weight is his delight.

Proverbs 11:1 KJV

LET US PRAISE GOD FOR HONEST FRIENDS.

Honesty has a beautiful and refreshing simplicity about it. No ulterior motives. No hidden meanings. As honesty and integrity characterize our lives, there will be no need to manipulate others.

Chuck Swindoll

Integrity is not a given factor in everyone's life. It is a result of self-discipline, inner trust, and a decision to be relentlessly honest in all situations in our lives.

John Maxwell

Dear Heavenly Father,

Thank You for trustworthy friends; let me, in turn, be a trustworthy friend to them. Lord, You have commanded Your children to walk in truth. Let me seek the truth and speak the truth, today and every day of my life.

Amen

Hope

But as for me, I will always have hope; I will praise you more and more.

Psalm 71:14 NIV

Be kindly affectioned one to another with brotherly love; in honor preferring one another; not slothful in business; fervent in spirit; serving the Lord; rejoicing in hope; patient in tribulation; continuing instant in prayer....

Romans 12:10-12 KJV

May the God of hope fill you with all joy and peace as you trust in him, so that you may overflow with hope by the power of the Holy Spirit.

Romans 15:13 NIV

Know that wisdom is sweet to your soul; if you find it, there is a future hope for you, and your hope will not be cut off.

Proverbs 24:14 NIV

LET US PRAISE GOD IN A SPIRIT OF HOPEFULNESS.

Hope is no other than the expectation of those things which faith has believed to be truly promised by God.

John Calvin

The choice for me is to either look at all things I have lost or the things I have. To live in fear or to live in hope.... Hope comes from knowing I have a sovereign, loving God who is in every event in my life.

Lisa Beamer
(Her husband Todd was killed on flight 93, 9-11-01)

Dear Heavenly Father,

Today I will live in hope. If I become discouraged, I will turn to You. If I grow weary, I will seek strength in You. In every aspect of my life, I will trust You, and I will encourage others to do the same. You are my Father, Lord, and I place my hope and my faith in You.

Amen

Humility

Yea, all of you be subject one to another, and be clothed with humility: for God resisteth the proud, and giveth grace to the humble.

1 Peter 5:5 KJV

Who is wise and understanding among you? Let him show it by his good life, by deeds done in the humility that comes from wisdom.

James 3:13 NIV

Don't be selfish....Be humble, thinking of others as better than yourself.

Philippians 2:3 TLB

Though the Lord is great, he cares for the humble, but he keeps his distance from the proud.

Psalm 138:6 NLT

LET US PRAISE GOD HUMBLY.

We are never stronger than the moment we admit we are weak.

Beth Moore

It was pride that changed angels into devils; it is humility that makes men as angels.

Saint Augustine

A humble heart is like a magnet that draws the favor of God toward us.

Jim Cymbala

Dear Heavenly Father,

Jesus clothed Himself with humility when He chose to leave heaven and come to earth to live and die for us, His children. Jesus is my Master and my example. Clothe me with humility, Lord, so that I might be more like Your Son.

Amen

Jesus

I am the door: by me if any man enter in, he shall be saved, and shall go in and out, and find pasture.

John 10:9 KJV

Jesus answered, "I am the way and the truth and the life. No one comes to the Father except through me. If you really knew me, you would know my Father as well. From now on, you do know him and have seen him."

John 14:6-7 NIV

At the name of Jesus every knee should bow, of things in heaven, and things in earth, and things under the earth; and that every tongue should confess that Jesus Christ is Lord, to the glory of God the Father.

Philippians 2:10-11 KJV

LET US PRAISE GOD FOR THE GIFT OF HIS SON.

All hail the power of Jesus' name! Let angels prostrate fall; bring forth the royal diadem, and crown Him Lord of all....

Edward Perronet

Jesus: the proof of God's love.

Philip Yancey

We accept Jesus Christ, the living Word of God, as our life.

Richard Foster

Dear Heavenly Father,

Thank You for Your Son Jesus, the Savior of my life. You loved this world so dearly, Father, that You sent Your Son to die so that we, Your children, might have life eternal. Let me always count Jesus as my dearest friend, and let me share His transforming message with a world in desperate need of His peace.

Amen

Joy

But let all who take refuge in you be glad; let them sing for joy. Spread your protection over them, that those who love your name may rejoice in you.

Psalm 5:11 NIV

So now we can rejoice in our wonderful new relationship with God—all because of what our Lord Jesus Christ has done for us in making us friends of God.

Romans 5:11 NLT

I will thank you, Lord, with all my heart; I will tell of all the marvelous things you have done. I will be filled with joy because of you. I will sing praises to your name, O Most High.

Psalm 9:1-2 NLT

Rejoice, and be exceeding glad: for great is your reward in heaven....

Matthew 5:12 KJV

LET US PRAISE GOD FOR THE JOY WE FEEL IN OUR HEARTS.

───────────◆───────────

Happy day, when Jesus washed my sins away! He taught me how to watch and pray and live rejoicing every day.

Philip Doddridge

To choose joy means the determination to let whatever takes place bring us one step closer to the God of life.

Henri Nouwen

Dear Heavenly Father,

You have told me to give thanks always and to rejoice in Your marvelous creation. Let me be a joyful Christian, Lord, and let me focus my thoughts upon Your blessings and Your Love. Help me make this day and every day a cause for celebration and praise as I share the Good News of Your Son.

Amen

Kindness of Friends

And above all things have fervent charity among yourselves: for charity shall cover the multitude of sins.

1 Peter 4:8 KJV

And be ye kind one to another, tenderhearted, forgiving one another, even as God for Christ's sake hath forgiven you.

Ephesians 4:32 KJV

Carry each other's burdens, and in this way you will fulfill the law of Christ.

Galatians 6:2 NIV

A gentle answer turns away wrath, but a harsh word stirs up anger.

Proverbs 15:1 NIV

LET US PRAISE GOD FOR
THE KINDNESS OF OTHERS.

While great brilliance and intellect are to be admired, they cannot dry one tear or mend a broken spirit. Only kindness can accomplish this.

John M. Drescher

Oh the comfort, the inexpressible comfort of feeling safe with a person; having neither to weigh thoughts nor measure words but to pour them all out, just as it is, chaff and grain together, knowing that a faithful hand will take and sift them, keeping what is worth keeping, and then, with the breath of kindness, blow the rest away.

Marian Evans

Dear Heavenly Father,

Thank you for the kindness of friends. You have brought loving friends and family members into my life. Let me return their kindness and their love. I praise You, Father, for the dear people who have enriched my life; may I, in turn, enrich theirs.

Amen

Kindness to Others

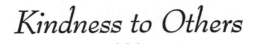

Be gentle unto all men, apt to teach, patient.

2 Timothy 2:24 KJV

A kind man benefits himself, but a cruel man brings trouble on himself.

Proverbs 11:17 NIV

Love one another deeply, from the heart.

1 Peter 1:22 NIV

I tell you the truth, whatever you did for one of the least of these brothers of mine, you did for me.

Matthew 25:40 NIV

Above all, love each other deeply, because love covers a multitude of sins.

1 Peter 4:8 NIV

LET US PRAISE GOD BY SHOWING KINDNESS TO OTHERS.

Do all the good you can. By all the means you can. In all the ways you can. In all the places you can. At all the times you can. To all the people you can. As long as ever you can.

John Wesley

When you extend hospitality to others, you're not trying to impress people; you're trying to reflect God to them.

Max Lucado

Dear Heavenly Father,

Help me to see the needs of those around me. Today, let me spread kind words of thanksgiving and celebration to friends and family. Today, let forgiveness rule my heart. And every day, Lord, let my love for Christ be reflected through deeds of kindness for those who need the healing touch of the Master's hand.

Amen

Laughter

Nehemiah said, "Go and enjoy choice food and sweet drinks, and send some to those who have nothing prepared. This day is sacred to our Lord. Do not grieve, for the joy of the LORD is your strength."

Nehemiah 8:10 NIV

A happy heart makes the face cheerful....

Proverbs 15:13 NIV

Clap your hands, all you nations; shout to God with cries of joy.

Psalm 47:1 NIV

Shout for joy to the LORD, all the earth, burst into jubilant song with music; make music to the LORD with the harp, with the harp and the sound of singing, with trumpets and the blast of the ram's horn—shout for joy before the LORD, the King.

Psalm 98:4-6 NIV

LET US PRAISE GOD FOR THE GIFT OF LAUGHTER.

———◈———

Laughter dulls the sharpest pain and flattens out the greatest stress. To share it is to give a gift of health.

Barbara Johnson

Humor is a prelude to faith, and laughter is the beginning of prayer.

Reinhold Niebuhr

It is often just as sacred to laugh as it is to pray.

Chuck Swindoll

Dear Heavenly Father,

When I begin to take myself or my life too seriously, let me laugh. When I rush from place to place, slow me down, Lord, and let me laugh. Put a smile on my face, Dear Lord, and let me share that smile with all who cross my path...and let me laugh.

Amen

Life

For whoever finds me finds life and receives favor from the LORD.

Proverbs 8:35 NIV

Thou wilt show me the path of life: in thy presence is fulness of joy; at thy right hand there are pleasures for evermore.

Psalm 16:11 KJV

Show me, O LORD, my life's end and the number of my days; let me know how fleeting is my life. You have made my days a mere hand-breadth; the span of my years is as nothing before you. Each man's life is but a breath.

Psalm 39:4 NIV

The fundamental fact of existence is that this trust in God, this faith, is the firm foundation under everything that makes life worth living.

Hebrews 11:1 MSG

LET US PRAISE GOD FOR THE GIFT OF LIFE.

I live because He is risen; I live to worship Him. Thank You, Jesus; because You're alive, I live!

Rich Cook

People, places, and things were never meant to give us life. God alone is the author of a fulfilling life.

Gary Smalley & John Trent

We die daily. Happy are those who daily come to life as well.

George MacDonald

Dear Heavenly Father,

You are the Giver of all Life, and You created me to have fellowship with You. Let me live a life that pleases You, Lord, and let me thank You always for Your blessings. You love me and protect me, Heavenly Father. Let me be grateful, and let me live for You today and throughout eternity.

Amen

Loving God

If you love me, you will obey what I command.

John 14:15 NIV

Jesus replied, "'Love the Lord your God with all your heart and with all your soul and with all your mind.' This is the first and greatest commandment. And the second is like it: 'Love your neighbor as yourself.' All the Law and the Prophets hang on these two commandments."

Matthew 22:37-40 NIV

It is good to praise the LORD and make music to your name, O Most High, to proclaim your love in the morning and your faithfulness at night....

Psalm 92:1-2 NIV

I love you, O LORD, my strength.

Psalm 18:1 NIV

LET US PRAISE GOD BY LOVING HIM.

———◈———

Joyful, joyful, we adore Thee, God of glory, Lord of love; Hearts unfold like flowers before Thee, opening to the sun above.

Henry van Dyke

Delighting thyself in the Lord is the sudden realization that He has become the desire of your heart.

Beth Moore

A man's spiritual health is exactly proportional to his love for God.

C. S. Lewis

Dear Heavenly Father,

You have blessed me with a love that is infinite and eternal. Let me love You, Lord, more and more each day. Make me a loving servant, Father, today and throughout eternity. And, let me demonstrate my praise for You by sharing Your message and Your love with others.

Amen

Loving Others

Above all, love each other deeply, because love covers a multitude of sins.

1 Peter 4:8 NIV

And just as you want men to treat you, treat them in the same way.

Luke 6:31 NASB

Let's see how inventive we can be in encouraging love and helping out, not avoiding worshipping together as some do but spurring each other on.

Hebrews 10:24-25 MSG

This is my commandment, That ye love one another, as I have loved you. Greater love hath no man than this, that a man lay down his life for his friends.

John 15:12-13 KJV

LET US PRAISE GOD BY SHOWING OUR LOVE FOR OTHERS.

They'll know we are Christians by our love.

Peter Scholtes

Brotherly love is still the distinguishing badge of every true Christian.

Matthew Henry

There is nothing that makes us love someone so much as praying for them.

William Law

Dear Heavenly Father,

You have given me love that is beyond human understanding, and I am Your loving servant. May the love that I feel for You be reflected in the compassion that I show to my family, to my friends, and to all who cross my path.

Amen

Miracles

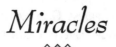

Jesus looked at them and said, "With man this is impossible, but with God all things are possible."

Matthew 19:26 NIV

You are the God who performs miracles; you display your power among the peoples.

Psalm 77:14 NIV

God also testified to it [salvation] by signs, wonders and various miracles, and gifts of the Holy Spirit distributed according to his will.

Hebrews 2:4 NIV

Jesus said to them, "I have shown you many great miracles from the Father."

John 10:32 NIV

For with God nothing shall be impossible.

Luke 1:37 KJV

LET US PRAISE GOD FOR HIS MIRACLES.

We have a God who delights in impossibilities.

Andrew Murray

The impossible is exactly what God does.

Oswald Chambers

Miracles broke the physical laws of the universe; forgiveness broke the moral rules.

Philip Yancey

Dear Heavenly Father,

You are the miracle worker of life; let me trust in Your power and Your love. With You, Father, all things are possible. Keep me mindful that You are a God of power and possibilities, and let me never place any limitations upon You, the Designer and Creator of the Universe.

Amen

Obedience

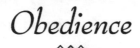

But if anyone obeys his word, God's love is truly made complete in him. This is how we know we are in him: Whoever claims to live in him must walk as Jesus did.

1 John 2:5-6 NIV

It is the LORD your God you must follow, and him you must revere. Keep his commands and obey him; serve him and hold fast to him.

Deuteronomy 13:4 NIV

Children, obey your parents in the Lord, for this is right.

Ephesians 6:1 NIV

Whatever you have learned or received or heard from me, or seen in me—put it into practice. And the God of peace will be with you.

Philippians 4:9 NIV

LET US PRAISE GOD BY BEING OBEDIENT TO HIS COMMANDMENTS.

All to Jesus I surrender, all to Him I freely give. I will ever love and trust Him, in His presence daily give.

Judson W. Van De Venter

There are two things we are called to do: we are to depend on His strength and be obedient to His Word. If we can't handle being dependent and obedient…we will never become the kind of people who have a heart for God.

Stuart Briscoe

Dear Heavenly Father,

When I turn my thoughts away from You and Your Word, I suffer. But when I obey Your commandments, when I place my faith in You, I am secure. Let me live according to Your commandments. Direct my path far from the temptations and distractions of this world. And, let me discover Your will and follow it, Dear Lord, this day and always.

Amen

Optimism

The Lord is my light and my salvation; whom shall I fear? The Lord is the strength of my life; of whom shall I be afraid?

Psalm 27:1 KJV

Finally, brethren, whatsoever things are true, whatsoever things are honest, whatsoever things are just, whatsoever things are pure, whatsoever things are lovely, whatsoever things are of good report; if there be any virtue, and if there be any praise, think on these things.

Philippians 4:8 KJV

Be of good courage, and he shall strengthen your heart, all ye that hope in the LORD.

Psalm 31:24 KJV

Make me to hear joy and gladness....

Psalm 51:8 KJV

LET US PRAISE GOD WITH EXPECTANT HEARTS.

Go forward confidently, energetically attacking problems, expecting favorable outcomes.

Norman Vincent Peale

Keep your feet on the ground, but let your heart soar as high as it will. Refuse to be average or to surrender to the chill of your spiritual environment.

A. W. Tozer

Think of the deliverance as well as the danger.

Thomas Fuller

Dear Heavenly Father,

Let me be an expectant Christian. Let me expect the best from You, and let me look for the best in others. If I become discouraged, Father, turn my thoughts and my prayers to You. Let me trust You, Lord, to direct my life. And, let me be Your faithful, hopeful, optimistic servant every day that I live.

Amen

Patience

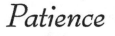

A man's wisdom gives him patience; it is to his glory to overlook an offense.

Proverbs 19:11 NIV

Wait patiently on the Lord. Be brave and courageous. Yes, wait patiently on the Lord.

Psalm 27:14 NLT

Be joyful in hope, patient in affliction, faithful in prayer.

Romans 12:12 NIV

Wait on the LORD, and he shall save thee.

Proverbs 20:22 KJV

The Lord is wonderfully good to those who wait for him and seek him. So it is good to wait quietly for salvation from the Lord.

Lamentations 3:25-26 NLT

LET US PRAISE GOD WITH PATIENT HEARTS.

Teach us, O Lord, the disciplines of patience, for to wait is often harder than to work.

Peter Marshall

God often permits us to be perplexed so that we may learn patience.

T.J. Bach

In the Bible, patience is not a passive acceptance of circumstances. It is a courageous perseverance in the face of suffering and difficulty.

Warren Wiersbe

Dear Heavenly Father,

Let me live according to Your plan and according to Your timetable. When I am hurried, Lord, slow me down. When I become impatient with others, give me empathy. Today, Lord, let me be a patient Christian, and let me trust in You and in Your master plan.

Amen

Peace

Be perfect, be of good comfort, be of one mind, live in peace; and the God of love and peace shall be with you.

2 Corinthians 13:11 KJV

And let the peace of God rule in your hearts… and be ye thankful.

Colossians 3:15 KJV

And the seed whose fruit is righteousness is sown in peace by those who make peace.

James 3:18 NASB

Peace I leave with you, my peace I give unto you: not as the world giveth, give I unto you. Let not your heart be troubled, neither let it be afraid.

John 14:27 KJV

LET US PRAISE GOD FOR THE PEACE HE OFFERS US.

Lord, dismiss us with Thy blessing; fill our hearts with joy and peace. Let us each, Thy love possessing, triumph in redeeming grace.

John Fawcett

Christ alone can bring lasting peace—peace with God—peace among men and nations—and peace within our hearts.

Billy Graham

Peace with God is where all peace begins.

Jim Gallery

Dear Heavenly Father,

The peace that the world offers is fleeting, but You offer a peace that is perfect and eternal. Let me turn the cares and burdens of my life over to You, Father, and let me feel the spiritual abundance that You offer through the person of Your Son, the Prince of Peace.

Amen

Perseverance

━━━━━◆━━━━━

Thanks be to God! He gives us the victory through our Lord Jesus Christ. Therefore, my dear brothers, stand firm. Let nothing move you. Always give yourselves fully to the work of the Lord, because you know that your labor in the Lord is not in vain.

1 Corinthians 15:57-58 NIV

Let us not become weary in doing good, for at the proper time we will reap a harvest if we do not give up.

Galatians 6:9 NIV

I have fought a good fight, I have finished my course, I have kept the faith.

2 Timothy 4:7 KJV

Consider it pure joy, my brothers, whenever you face trials of many kinds, because you know that the testing of your faith develops perseverance.

James 1:2-3 NIV

LET US PRAISE GOD WITH PERSEVERANCE AND DETERMINATION.

By perseverance, the snail reached the ark.

C. H. Spurgeon

Keep adding, keep walking, keep advancing; do not stop, do not turn back, do not turn from the straight road.

Saint Augustine

Jesus taught that perseverance is the essential element in prayer.

E. M. Bounds

Dear Heavenly Father,

Sometimes, life is difficult indeed. Sometimes, we are burdened or fearful. Sometimes, we cry tears of bitterness or loss, but even then, You never leave our sides. Today, Lord, let me be a finisher of my faith. Let me persevere—even if the day is difficult—and let me help my family and friends trust in Your infinite strength and in Your infinite love.

Amen

Prayer

If my people who are called by my name, will humble themselves and pray and seek my face and turn from their wicked ways, then will I hear from heaven and will forgive their sin and will heal their land.

2 Chronicles 7:14 NIV

The effective prayer of a righteous man can accomplish much.

James 5:16 NASB

And it will come about that whoever calls on the name of the LORD will be delivered.

Joel 2:32 NASB

I sought the LORD, and he heard me, and delivered me from all my fears.

Psalm 34:4 KJV

LET US PRAISE GOD FOR THE GIFT OF PRAYER.

⎯⎯⎯⎯⎯◆⎯⎯⎯⎯⎯

I have been driven many times to my knees by the overwhelming conviction that I had absolutely no other place to go.

Abraham Lincoln

Prayer is conversation with God.

Clement of Alexandria

Any concern that is too small to be turned into a prayer is too small to be made into a burden.

Corrie ten Boom

Dear Heavenly Father,

Your Word commands me to pray without ceasing. Let me take everything to You in prayer. When I am discouraged, let me pray. When I grieve, let me take my tears to You. And when I am joyful, let me offer up prayers of thanksgiving. In all things great and small, at all times, whether happy or sad, let me seek Your wisdom and Your Grace . . . in prayer.

Amen

Renewal

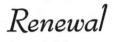

...inwardly we are being renewed day by day.

2 Corinthians 4:16 NIV

I will give you a new heart and put a new spirit in you....

Ezekiel 36:26 NIV

Remember ye not the former things, neither consider the things of old. Behold, I will do a new thing....

Isaiah 43:18-19 KJV

He restoreth my soul.

Psalm 23:3 KJV

And be not conformed to this world: but be ye transformed by the renewing of your mind.

Romans 12:2 KJV

LET US PRAISE GOD FOR THE RENEWAL HE OFFERS.

Repentance removes old sins and wrong attitudes, and it opens the way for the Holy Spirit to restore our spiritual health.

Shirley Dobson

He is the God of wholeness and restoration.

Stormie Omartian

God is not running an antique shop! He is making all things new!

Vance Havner

Dear Heavenly Father,

Sometimes I am troubled, and sometimes I grow weary. When I am weak, Lord, give me strength. When I am discouraged, renew me. When I am fearful, let me feel Your healing touch. Let me always trust in Your promises, Lord, and let me draw strength from those promises and from Your unending love.

Amen

Repentance

I preached that they should repent and turn to God and prove their repentance by their deeds.

Acts 26:20 NIV

Therefore this is what the Lord says: "If you repent, I will restore you that you may serve me...."

Jeremiah 15:19 NIV

The LORD is close to the brokenhearted and saves those who are crushed in spirit.

Psalm 34:18 NIV

But their scribes and Pharisees murmured against his disciples, saying, Why do ye eat and drink with publicans and sinners? And Jesus answering said unto them, They that are whole need not a physician; but they that are sick. I came not to call the righteous, but sinners to repentance.

Luke 5:30-32 KJV

L**ET US PRAISE** G**OD AND REPENT FROM EVIL.**

Repentance is the decision to turn from selfish desires and seek God. It is a genuine sorrow and moves us to admit wrong and desire to do better.

Max Lucado

Repentance becomes a way of life, a lifelong process of turning towards the Holy One, that happens one day at a time.

Trevor Hudson

But suppose we do sin. Suppose we slip and fall. Suppose we yield to temptation for a moment. What happens? We have to confess that sin.

Billy Graham

Dear Heavenly Father,

When I stray from Your commandments, I must not only confess my sins, but I must also turn from them. When I fall short, help me to change. When I reject Your Word and Your will for my life, guide me back to Your side. Your plan is perfect, Father; I am not. Let me trust in You.

Amen

Righteousness

—◈—

Blessed are those who hunger and thirst for righteousness, for they will be filled.

Matthew 5:6 NIV

Therefore everyone who hears these words of mine and puts them into practice is like a wise man who built his house on the rock. The rain came down, and the winds blew and beat against the house; yet it did not fall, because it had its foundation on the rock.

Matthew 7:24-25 NIV

The steps of a good man are ordered by the LORD....

Psalm 37:23 KJV

The Lord will not reject his people; he will not abandon his own special possession. Judgment will come again for the righteous, and those who are upright will have a reward.

Psalm 94:14-15 NLT

LET US PRAISE GOD BY LIVING RIGHTEOUS LIVES.

Have your heart right with Christ, and he will visit you often, and so turn weekdays into Sundays, meals into sacraments, homes into temples, and earth into heaven.

C. H. Spurgeon

A life lived in God is not lived on the plane of feelings, but of the will.

Elisabeth Elliot

A life growing in its purity and devotion will be a more prayerful life.

E. M. Bounds

Dear Heavenly Father,

This world is filled with many distractions and temptations. When I turn my thoughts away from You and Your Word, I suffer. But, when I trust in Your commandments, I am safe. Let me discover Your will and follow it, Father, and let me help my friends and family to do the same, this day and always.

Amen

Salvation

And we have seen and testify that the Father has sent his Son to be the Savior of the world.

1 John 4:14 NIV

It is a trustworthy statement, deserving full acceptance, that Christ Jesus came into the world to save sinners....

1 Timothy 1:15 NASB

Whosoever transgresseth, and abideth not in the doctrine of Christ, hath not God. He that abideth in the doctrine of Christ, he hath both the Father and the Son.

2 John 9 KJV

In that day they will say, "Surely this is our God; we trusted in him, and he saved us. This is the LORD, we trusted in him; let us rejoice and be glad in his salvation."

Isaiah 25:9 NIV

LET US PRAISE GOD FOR THE GIFT OF SALVATION.

———————◆◆◆———————

Rock of ages, cleft for me, let me hide myself in thee; let the water and the blood, from Thy wounded side which flowed, be of sin the double cure, save from wrath and make me pure.

Augustus M. Toplady

The amazing thing about Jesus is that He doesn't just patch up our lives; He gives us a brand new sheet, a clean slate to start over, all new.

Gloria Gaither

Dear Heavenly Father,

My salvation is in You. My soul finds rest in You through Your Son Jesus Christ. The gift of salvation brings meaning to my life here on earth just as surely as it prepares me for eternal life with You in heaven. Let me praise You and give thanks for Your glorious gift...and let me share it with all who cross my path.

Amen

Seeking God

God did this so that men would seek him and perhaps reach out for him and find him, though he is not far from each one of us.

Acts 17:27 NIV

But if from there you seek the LORD your God, you will find him if you look for him with all your heart and with all your soul.

Deuteronomy 4:29 NIV

You will seek me and find me when you seek me with all your heart.

Jeremiah 29:13 NIV

I seek you with all my heart; do not let me stray from your commands.

Psalm 119:10 NIV

LET US PRAISE GOD BY SEEKING HIM.

To have found God and still to pursue Him is the soul's paradox of love.

A. W. Tozer

Let us humble our hearts before the Lord and seek his help and approval above all other things.

Jim Cymbala

We rarely discover anything monumental about God without discovering something momentous about ourselves. With every revelation comes an invitation to adjust out lives to what we have seen.

Beth Moore

Dear Heavenly Father,

How comforting it is to know that if I seek You, I will find You. You are with me, Father, every step that I take. Let me reach out to You, and let me praise You for revealing Your Word, Your way, and Your love.

Amen

Serving God

So then, men ought to regard us as servants of Christ and as those entrusted with the secret things of God. Now it is required that those who have been given a trust must prove faithful.

I Corinthians 4:1-2 NIV

Serve wholeheartedly, as if you were serving the Lord, not men.

Ephesians 6:7 NIV

Choose you this day whom ye will serve…as for me and my house, we will serve the LORD.

Joshua 24:15 KJV

His master replied, "Well done, good and faithful servant! You have been faithful with a few things; I will put you in charge of many things. Come and share your master's happiness!"

Matthew 25:21 NIV

LET US PRAISE GOD BY SERVING HIM.

———————◇———————

Ye servants of God, your Master proclaim, and publish abroad His wonderful name.

Charles Wesley

We are finding we don't have such a gnawing need to know the answers when we know the Answer.

Gloria Gaither

In the great orchestra we call life, you have an instrument and a song, and you owe it to God to play them both sublimely.

Max Lucado

Dear Heavenly Father,

Let me serve You and follow Your commandments. When I am tempted to stray from Your Word and from Your will, direct my thoughts back to You. Lead me far from temptation, Lord, so that I might serve You and only You.

Amen

Serving Others

◆

Whatever you do, work at it with all your heart, as working for the Lord, not for men, since you know that you will receive an inheritance from the Lord as a reward. It is the Lord Christ you are serving.

Colossians 3:23-24 NIV

Suppose a brother or a sister is without clothes and daily food. If one of you says to him, "Go, I wish you well; keep warm and well fed," but does nothing about his physical needs, what good is it?

James 2:15-16 NIV

A generous man will prosper; he who refreshes others will himself be refreshed.

Proverbs 11:25 NIV

Be devoted to one another in brotherly love. Honor one another above yourselves.

Romans 12:10 NIV

LET US PRAISE GOD BY SERVING OTHERS.

Do things for others and you'll find your self-consciousness evaporating like morning dew on a Missouri cornfield in July.

Dale Carnegie

Carve your name on hearts, not on marble.

C. H. Spurgeon

If the attitude of servanthood is learned, by attending to God as Lord, then serving others will develop as a very natural way of life.

Eugene Peterson

Dear Heavenly Father,

When Jesus humbled Himself and became a servant, He also became an example for His followers. Today, as I serve my family and friends, I do so in the name of Jesus. Guide my steps, Father, and let my service be pleasing to You.

Amen

Spiritual Growth

Do not store up for yourselves treasures on earth, where moth and rust destroy, and where thieves break in and steal. But store up for yourselves treasures in heaven, where moth and rust do not destroy, and where thieves do not break in and steal. For where your treasure is, there your heart will be also.

Matthew 6:19-21 NIV

Long for the pure milk of the word, so that by it you may grow in respect to salvation.

1 Peter 2:2 NASB

Know the love of Christ which surpasses knowledge, that you may be filled up to all the fullness of God.

Ephesians 3:19 NASB

But grow in the grace and knowledge of our Lord and Savior Jesus Christ. To Him be the glory, both now and to the day of eternity.

2 Peter 3:18 NASB

132

LET US PRAISE GOD BY GROWING IN THE KNOWLEDGE
OF HIS WORD AND HIS WILL.

———————————◆◆◆———————————

Growing in any area of the Christian life takes time, and the key is daily sitting at the feet of Jesus.

Cynthia Heald

The vigor of our spiritual lives will be in exact proportion to the place held by the Bible in our lives and in our thoughts

George Müller

There will be times when we come to God, listen to Him, and then grapple with what we hear.

Charles Stanley

Dear Heavenly Father,

When I open myself to You, I am blessed. Let me accept Your love and Your wisdom, Father. Show me Your way, and deliver me from the painful mistakes that I make when I stray from Your commandments. Let me live according to Your Word, and let me grow in my faith every day that I live.

Amen

Strength

Those who hope in the LORD will renew their strength. They will soar on wings like eagles; they will run and not grow weary, they will walk and not be faint.

Isaiah 40:31 NIV

I can do all things through Him who strengthens me.

Philippians 4:13 NASB

He said unto me, My grace is sufficient for thee: for my strength is made perfect in weakness.

2 Corinthians 12:9 KJV

Whatever your hand finds to do, do it with all your might....

Ecclesiastes 9:10 NIV

The LORD is my strength and my song....

Exodus 15:2 NIV

Let us praise God for the strength He gives us.

———◆———

Jesus is all the world to me, my life, my joy, my all; He is my strength from day to day, without Him I would fall.

Will L. Thompson

Worry does not empty tomorrow of its sorrow; it empties today of its strength.

Corrie ten Boom

The more I have, the less I depend on him. And as I grasp how truly poor and needy I am, then I can let God's power come to full strength in me.

Ronald Wilson

Dear Heavenly Father,

Sometimes life is difficult. Sometimes, I am worried, weary, or heartbroken. But, when I lift my eyes to You, Father, You strengthen me. When I am weak, You lift me up. Today, I turn to You, Lord, for my strength, for my hope, and my salvation.

Amen

Talents

Do not neglect the spiritual gift that is within you....

1 Timothy 4:14 NASB

Each man has his own gift from God; one has this gift, another has that.

1 Corinthians 7:7 NIV

Neglect not the gift that is in thee....

1 Timothy 4:14 KJV

I remind you to fan into flame the gift of God.

2 Timothy 1:6 NIV

Every good gift and every perfect gift is from above, and cometh down from the Father of lights.

James 1:17 KJV

LET US PRAISE GOD FOR OUR TALENTS.

One thing taught large in the Holy Scriptures is that while God gives His gifts freely, He will require a strict accounting of them at the end of the road. Each man is personally responsible for his store, be it large or small, and will be required to explain his use of it before the judgment seat of Christ.

A. W. Tozer

What we are is God's gift to us. What we become is our gift to God.

Eleanor Powell

Dear Heavenly Father,

You have given me abilities to be used for the glory of Your kingdom. Give me the courage and the perseverance to use those talents. Keep me mindful that all my gifts come from You, Lord. Let me be Your faithful, humble servant, and let me give You all the glory and all the praise.

Amen

Temptation

No temptation has seized you except what is common to man. And God is faithful; he will not let you be tempted beyond what you can bear. But when you are tempted, he will also provide a way out so that you can stand up under it.

I Corinthians 10:13 NIV

Watch and pray so that you will not fall into temptation. The spirit is willing but the body is weak.

Matthew 26:41 NIV

Your adversary, the devil, prowls around like a roaring lion, seeking someone to devour.

I Peter 5:8 NASB

The Lord knoweth how to deliver the godly out of temptation....

2 Peter 2:9 KJV

LET US PRAISE GOD WHEN HE LEADS US
FAR FROM TEMPTATION.

Jesus faced every temptation known to humanity so that He could identify with us.

Beth Moore

Man without God is always torn between two urges. His nature prompts him to do wrong, and his conscience urges him to do right. Christ can rid you of that inner conflict.

Billy Graham

Dear Heavenly Father,

This world is filled with many temptations, distractions, and frustrations. When I turn my thoughts away from You and Your Word, Lord, I suffer bitter consequences. But, when I trust in Your commandments, I am safe. Direct my path far from the temptations and distractions of the world. Let me discover Your will and follow it, Dear Lord, this day and always.

Amen

Testimony

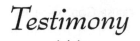

Sanctify the Lord God in your hearts: and be ready always to give an answer to every man that asketh you a reason of the hope that is in you....

1 Peter 3:15 KJV

For God has not given us a spirit of timidity, but of power and love and discipline. Therefore do not be ashamed of the testimony of our Lord....

2 Timothy 1:7-8 NASB

Whoever acknowledges me before men, I will also acknowledge him before my Father in heaven.

Matthew 10:32 NIV

You are the light of the world.

Matthew 5:14 NIV

LET US PRAISE GOD BY SHARING OUR TESTIMONIES.

Brother, sister, let me serve you, let me be as Christ to you; pray that I may have the grace to let you be my servant, too.

Richard Gillard

Every believer may be brought to understand that the only object of his life is to help to make Christ King on the earth.

Andrew Murray

Winning the world to Christ means winning individuals.

Erwin Lutzer

Dear Heavenly Father,

The life that I live and the words that I speak bear testimony to my faith. Make me a faithful servant of Your Son, and let my testimony be worthy of You. Let my words be sure and true, Lord, and let my actions point others to You.

Amen

Thanksgiving

Give thanks in all circumstances; for this is God's will for you in Christ Jesus.

1 Thessalonians 5:18 NIV

Is anyone happy? Let him sing songs of praise.

James 5:13 NIV

Make a joyful noise unto the Lord all ye lands. Serve the Lord with gladness: come before his presence with singing. Know ye that the Lord he is God: it is he that hath made us, and not we ourselves; we are his people and the sheep of his pasture. Enter into his gates with thanksgiving, and into his courts with praise; be thankful unto him and bless his name. For the Lord is good; his mercy is everlasting; and his truth endureth to all generations.

Psalm 100 KJV

LET US PRAISE GOD WITH THANKSGIVING
IN OUR HEARTS.

Rejoice, ye pure in heart; rejoice, give thanks, and sing. Your festal banner wave on high-the cross of Christ, your King.

Edward H. Plumptre

God is worthy of our praise and is pleased when we come before Him with thanksgiving.

Shirley Dobson

We should spend as much time in thanking God for his benefits as we do asking him for them.

St. Vincent de Paul

Dear Heavenly Father,

Your gifts are greater than I can imagine. May I live each day with thanksgiving in my heart and praise on my lips. Thank You for the gift of Your Son and for the promise of eternal life. Let me share the joyous news of Jesus Christ with my friends and my family, and let my life be a testimony to His love and to His grace.

Amen

Today

Encourage one another daily, as long as it is Today....

Hebrews 3:13 NIV

Choose for yourselves this day whom you will serve...as for me and my household, we will serve the LORD.

Joshua 24:15 NIV

Give your entire attention to what God is doing right now, and don't get worked up about what may or may not happen tomorrow. God will help you deal with whatever hard things come up when the time comes.

Matthew 6:33-34 MSG

This is the day the LORD has made; let us rejoice and be glad in it.

Psalm 118:24 NIV

LET US PRAISE GOD FOR THIS DAY.

Wherever you are, be all there. Live to the hilt every situation you believe to be the will of God.

Jim Elliot

Love, joy, peace, patience, kindness, goodness, faithfulness, gentleness, and self-control. To these I commit my day. If I succeed, I will give thanks. If I fail, I will seek his grace. And then, when this day is done, I will place my head on my pillow and rest.

Max Lucado

Dear Heavenly Father,

This is the day that You have given me. Let me be thankful, and let me use it according to Your plan. I praise You, Father, for the gift of life and for the friends and family members who make my life rich. Enable me to live each moment to the fullest, totally involved in Your will.

Amen

Trust in God

❖

Do not let your hearts be troubled. Trust in God; trust also in me. In my Father's house are many rooms; if it were not so, I would have told you. I am going there to prepare a place for you.

John 14:1-2 NIV

Fear of man will prove to be a snare, but whoever trusts in the LORD is kept safe.

Proverbs 29:25 NIV

For the Lord God is our light and our protector. He gives us grace and glory. No good thing will the Lord withhold from those who do what is right. O Lord Almighty, happy are those who trust in you.

Psalm 84:11-12 NLT

He heeded their prayer, because they put their trust in him.

1 Chronicles 5:20 NKJV

LET US PRAISE GOD BY TRUSTING HIM.

———◆———

'Tis sweet to trust in Jesus, just to take Him at His Word; just to rest upon His promise, just to know, "Thus saith the Lord."

Louisa M. R. Snead

Friend, you can trust the Man that died for you.

James McConkey

Trusting God is the bottom line of Christian righteousness.

R. C. Sproul

Dear Heavenly Father,

When I trust in things of this earth, I will be disappointed. But, when I put my faith in You, I am secure. You are my rock and my shield. Upon Your firm foundation I will build my life. You will love me and protect me, and You will share Your boundless grace today, tomorrow, and forever.

Amen

Truth

Buy the truth and do not sell it; get wisdom, discipline, and understanding.

Proverbs 23:23 NIV

These are the things you are to do: Speak the truth to each other, and render true and sound judgment in your courts....

Zechariah 8:16 NIV

Therefore laying aside falsehood, speak truth, each one of you, with his neighbor, for we are members of one another.

Ephesians 4:25 NASB

Jesus answered, "I am the way and the truth and the life. No one comes to the Father except through me."

John 14:6 NIV

LET US PRAISE GOD FOR HIS TRUTH.

━━━━━━━━◇◆◇━━━━━━━━

I would rather know the truth than be happy in ignorance. If I cannot have both truth and happiness, give me truth. We'll have a long time to be happy in heaven.

A. W. Tozer

God offers to everyone the choice between truth and repose. Take which you please—you can never have both.

Ralph Waldo Emerson

Dear Heavenly Father,

You are a God of truth, and You command Your children to walk in truth. Let me follow Your commandment. Let me walk righteously with You so that others might see Your eternal truth reflected in my words and my deeds.

Amen

Wisdom

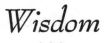

Let the word of Christ dwell in you richly in all wisdom; teaching and admonishing one another in psalms and hymns and spiritual songs, singing with grace in your hearts to the Lord.

Colossians 3:16 KJV

Those who are wise will shine like the brightness of the heavens, and those who lead many to righteousness, like the stars for ever and ever.

Daniel 12:3 NIV

If any of you lack wisdom, let him ask of God, that giveth to all men liberally, and upbraideth not; and it shall be given him.

James 1:5 KJV

He who walks with the wise grows wise....

Proverbs 13:20 NIV

LET US PRAISE GOD FOR HIS WISDOM.

Knowledge is horizontal. Wisdom is vertical; it comes down from above.

Billy Graham

The fruit of wisdom is Christlikeness, peace, humility, and love. And, the root of it is faith in Christ as the manifested wisdom of God.

J. I. Packer

If you lack knowledge, go to school. If you lack wisdom, get on your knees.

Vance Havner

Dear Heavenly Father,

I seek wisdom not as the world gives, but as You give. Lead me in Your ways and teach me from Your Word so that, in time, my wisdom might glorify Your kingdom, Lord, and Your Son.

Amen

Work

But as for you, be strong and do not give up, for your work will be rewarded.

2 Chronicles 15:7 NIV

Moreover, when God gives any man wealth and possessions, and enables him to enjoy them, to accept his lot and be happy in his work—this is a gift of God.

Ecclesiastes 5:19 NIV

Be kindly affectioned one to another with brotherly love; in honor preferring one another; not slothful in business; fervent in spirit; serving the Lord; rejoicing in hope; patient in tribulation; continuing instant in prayer....

Romans 12:10-12 KJV

The sleep of a labouring man is sweet....

Ecclesiastes 5:12 KJV

LET US PRAISE GOD BY WORKING DILIGENTLY.

───────────◇───────────

Ordinary work, which is what most of us do most of the time, is ordained by God every bit as much as is the extraordinary.

Elisabeth Elliot

I seem to have been led, little by little, toward my work; and I believe that the same fact will appear in the life of anyone who will cultivate such powers as God has given him and then go on, bravely, quietly, but persistently, doing such work as comes to his hands.

Fanny Crosby

Dear Heavenly Father,

I know that You desire a bountiful harvest for all Your children. But, You have instructed us that we must sow before we reap, not after. Help me, Lord, to sow the seeds of Your abundance everywhere I go. Let me be diligent in all my undertakings and give me patience to wait for Your harvest.

Amen

Worry

Let not your heart be troubled: ye believe in God, believe also in me.

John 14:1 KJV

Come to me, all you who are weary and burdened, and I will give you rest. Take my yoke upon you and learn from me, for I am gentle and humble in heart, and you will find rest for your souls. For my yoke is easy and my burden is light.

Matthew 11:28-30 NIV

Cast your burden upon the Lord and He will sustain you: He will never allow the righteous to be shaken.

Psalm 55:22 NASB

An anxious heart weighs a man down....

Proverbs 12:25 NIV

LET US PRAISE GOD BY TURNING OUR WORRIES OVER TO HIM.

———————◆————————

Don't let worry rob you of the joy that is rightfully yours. God is in heaven, and He knows your every need. Focus on God and His provisions, and watch gratefully as the worries of today begin to fade away.

Jim Gallery

Pray, and let God worry.

Martin Luther

Worry makes you forget who's in charge.

Max Lucado

Dear Heavenly Father,

Forgive me when I let my heart worry. Worry reflects a lack of trust in Your ability to meet my every need. Help me to work, Lord, and not to worry. And, keep me mindful, Father, that nothing, absolutely nothing, will happen this day that You and I cannot handle together.

Amen

Worship

You will be a good servant of Christ Jesus, constantly nourished on the words of the faith and of the sound doctrine which you have been following.

1 Timothy 4:6 NASB

God lifted him high and honored him far beyond anyone or anything, ever, so that all created beings in heaven and earth, even those long ago dead and buried, will bow in worship before this Jesus Christ, and call out in praise that he is the Master of all, to the glorious honor of God the Father.

Philippians 2:9-11 MSG

I was glad when they said to me, "Let us go to the house of the Lord."

Psalm 122:1 NLT

If any man thirst, let him come unto me, and drink.

John 7:37 KJV

LET US PRAISE GOD BY WORSHIPING HIM.

———◆———

You were Lord of the heavens before time was time, and Lord of all lords You will be! We bow down and we worship You, Lord.

Twila Paris

In Biblical worship you do not find the repetition of a phrase; instead, you find the worshipers rehearsing the character of God and His ways, reminding Him of His faithfulness and His wonderful promises.

Kay Arthur

Dear Heavenly Father,

This world is a place of distractions and temptations. But when I worship You, Father, You set my path—and my heart—straight. Let this day and every day be a time of worship. Whether I am in Your house or simply going about my daily activities, let me worship You, not only with words and deeds, but also with my heart.

Amen